Acting Edition

THE HALF-LIFE OF MARIE CURIE

BY LAUREN GUNDERSON

MUSIC AND THIRD-PARTY MATERIALS USE NOTE

IMPORTANT BILLING AND CREDIT REQUIREMENTS

THE HALF-LIFE OF MARIE CURIE was originally commissioned and produced by Audible Theater at the Minetta Lane Theatre on November 19, 2019, in New York City. It was directed by Gaye Taylor Upchurch, the set design was by Rachel Hauck, the costume design was by Sarah Laux, the lighting design was by Amith Chandrashaker, the sound design was by Darron L. West, and the production stage manager was Michelle Bosch. The cast was as follows:

MARIE CURIE .... Francesca Faridany
HERTHA AYRTON .... Kate Mulgrew

CHARACTERS

MARIE CURIE—44. Polish-born, French national. Brilliant, shrewd, private, and patient scientist. At this point she has already won her first Nobel Prize in Physics with her husband, Pierre, in 1903. She is the mother of two daughters, Irene (14) and Eve (7). She was widowed in 1906 when her husband died tragically.

HERTHA AYRTON—57. British. A brazen, ambitious, fiercely intelligent engineer, inventor, and suffragist. Widowed in 1908, she continued her work in electrical experimentation while secretly housing suffragettes running from police. Of Jewish origin, she became an agnostic pragmatist who changed her name from Sarah to Hertha after a Swinburne poem about a goddess of the earth.

SETTING

1911–1914, France and England.

"Science is always there, grand and calm, a refuge against all evils. That is what I feel when I settle into my laboratory and that is what Madame Curie must remember."

—Hertha Ayrton

"Marie Curie's gradual recovery should be credited largely to Hertha Ayrton, who offered Marie and her daughters sanctuary in England. Using her mother's name, Marie met Hertha at an old mill-house she had rented for the summer at Highcliffe-on-Sea in Hampshire. In addition to being a scientist of note, Ayrton was a superb nurse and a crusader for women's rights. […]
As Marie emerged from her mental and physical collapse, World War I began."

—*Obsessive Genius:*
The Inner World of Marie Curie
by Barbara Goldsmith

THE HALF-LIFE OF MARIE CURIE

Scene 1

1911.
Hertha's ode to the electric arc.

HERTHA. There was a technical problem in the world and I fixed it and you're welcome.

You see human beings are very clever, aren't we, and we invented electric lamps, and by 1890 there were such lamps on every street in London, lighting stages, warming dining rooms, isn't *that* lovely. Except no, no it was not lovely *it was loud.* The damn things made this hissing, scratching, popping noise and it was miserable. It was…well it was this:

We hear the clicking hiss of the electric lamps.

Isn't that the most dreadful thing you've ever heard! Good god. I'd rather go back to candles and shouting "*Where are you?!*" after dinner.

But the choice can't be: racket or *darkness.* So I ask myself, Why the hiss? Which was the right question to ask because it had an answer and I found it. The lamp is called an *arc* lamp because the electricity arced across a small divide in between two carbon rods. That's what makes the glow: the empty space between the rods, like fingertips nearly touching. Isn't that a lovely metaphor for—I don't care. Now, I figure out that the empty space also allows for oxygen to pool at the tip of the rods which promotes rapid heating, which promotes… that hiss.

That hiss again. Ugh.

So I redesigned the damn things and now they behave.

The hissing vanishes.

Listen to that.

We listen.

That's the sound of a good idea.
And as I said…you're welcome.

Blackout.

Marie's ode to the radium in her pocket.

MARIE. *(Holding, investigating the substance itself.)* Radium is a cold heat, a dark light, a force of nature. I have it with me now. *A vial in my pocket. I take it out. I hold it.* It glows. Turn down the light and one sees a watery, green…fire. No. It's more constant than a flame. A *gaze.* Like it can't take its eyes off you. Like the love of your life.

This is why I keep it with me. It reminds me of Pierre. Husband. Together we shoveled small mountains of pitchblende heaped in a sooty shed, dissolved it in acid, boiled it down, scraped the black bits to purify this element. Ten tons of the rock we shoveled distilled into just enough Radium to sprinkle on your fingertip. *That's* a certain kind of marriage, don't you think?

"Radioactive" is my word. I coined it. That was me. So…

Now it is *only* me. Pierre is dead, gone six years now, and I am alone and our girls are alone, and it is only me and the glow and the gaze of the element in my pocket.

You see radiation is the process by which an element changes itself entirely. As it radiates, Radium decays to Radon which decays to Polonium which decays to Lead, all of these metals shedding themselves to the point of abandonment. I empathize.

Half-life. The moment an element transforms so fully that it is more other than self. That's what we call it. Half…life.

We hear a low ticking…

Do you hear it? Radium and its half-life approaching.
Not everyone can hear it. But I can. I do.

Tick…tick…tick…

This is shattered by…or grows to become…

Scene 2

A mob outside of Marie Curie's door in Sceaux, France. Shouting, banging on the door. Someone throws something at the wall, at the window.

The door opens and the racket outside floods in. None louder than the woman entering, who bellows back at the masses.

HERTHA. You're nothing but a pack of wolves. Do you know whose house this is? Do you have any idea who *this great woman is*? Also there are children in this house and if you frighten them any more than you already have I swear to a god I don't believe in that I'll come to each one of your houses and SHAKE THEIR FOUNDATIONS.

    She slams the door.

Marie? Marie are you alright? // I'm here! It's me.

MARIE.   *Who's here? What's // going on?*

    HERTHA.   It's Hertha, my dear. // I'm here to help.

        MARIE.   What do you mean it's Hertha? Why?

            HERTHA.   Why what?

                MARIE.   Are you here?! *Why are you here?*

HERTHA. Because I thought I was going to very quietly make you tea and toast during your moderate troubles, but it looks like it'll be a bit more involved than that.
(Yelling through the window.) I SAID BACK OFF, YOU DOGS.
(Back to Marie.) How are you? May I come in? How are you?

MARIE. Oh I'm terrible, come in.

HERTHA. God, journalists are pigeons, you can't get rid of them before they shit on everything.

MARIE. I wish I'd known you were coming. We don't have much food or wine.

HERTHA. I told you I was coming. I wrote you five times.

MARIE. Five times?

HERTHA. When I didn't hear back I said, "Dammit now I'm nervous, I'll just get on a boat."

MARIE. I'm sorry. I stopped opening the mail. It's full of such loathing.

HERTHA. Task number one, then. Loathing has never had much effect on me. I'll go through the mail, I'll get food, I'll buy a saber of some sort to wave at those gossips.

Marie doesn't know what to do with this kindness.

MARIE. Thank you. You didn't have to come.

HERTHA. I know that. You didn't have to have an affair with Paul but you did. These things happen. We do things for people we love that make very little sense. And you love him, and I love you, so I got on a boat, punched a few journalists, and am now ready to comfort you. God, I'm furious about all this. I'm livid. I can't imagine what you're feeling.

MARIE. I might've finally *stopped* feeling actually. I can't decide if I'm shattered or slowly evaporating. I can hardly fathom that when they say "homewrecking harlot" they mean me.

HERTHA. Goddamn the press for doing this to you. They wouldn't do this to a man, you know. They aren't! I hear all manner of vileness about you, but Paul is called only an "unfaithful husband," and even that is said with a bit of congratulations.

MARIE. Even I look at what they write and think, "What a terrible woman that Madame Curie must be."

HERTHA. Don't you think that. Not for a minute.

MARIE. A minute can be such a long time.

HERTHA. Don't worry. I've already worked out a list of people to murder.

MARIE. Hertha.

HERTHA. It's not a *long* list.

MARIE. Don't even joke of such things.

HERTHA. Oh believe how seriously I would take it. I'm an engineer darling, we fix things any way we can. Now what else can I do? Tea? Coffee? Or I can start another list.

MARIE. I don't know, I don't know…anything. Every day it's not over it pulls me under a bit more. I'm starting to think I can't survive it.

HERTHA. Marie.

MARIE. Or that I shouldn't.

HERTHA. *Yes you damn well can and should.*

MARIE. *Not when they're dragging me and my girls deeper into hell each day.*
My girls, Hertha.
Nothing is worth this.

HERTHA. I know. I know that. That's why I'm here. How are the girls?

MARIE. They're trying to be strong but they don't know what to think.

HERTHA. Poor, sweet things. I'll distract them with suffragist ideology and chocolate.

MARIE. Can I have some chocolate too?

HERTHA. Only if you eat your dinner which will be steak because that's the only thing I really know how to cook. Good? Good.

MARIE. Paul is fighting a duel for me.

HERTHA. A what.

MARIE. A duel, I know.

HERTHA. With a weapon?

MARIE. Yes with a weapon, it's a duel.

HERTHA. I just hoped it was a maths duel or something. Who the hell is he dueling?

MARIE. One of the editors of these terrible papers. He's defending my honor, tomorrow in fact.

HERTHA. What an idiot. I'm sorry but he should stick to physics.

MARIE. *(Getting upset.)* I know. *I know.*

HERTHA. No, no, I'm sure he'll be fine. He'll be just fine.

MARIE. I know I'm not supposed to imagine a life with him but I do. He cannot die.

HERTHA. No no no. He won't die. French duels are mainly the *fashion* of guns not the *employment* of them. Not to worry. Nothing to worry about.

> *Marie cannot handle the thought. Hertha doesn't know how to help. We hear the tinkling of piano, a child is playing…*

Is that Evie? She plays so well for—what is she, seven now?

MARIE. Yes. The piano is the only thing that calms her. And me.

HERTHA. And they're not in school?

MARIE. There's so much fuss. They're too scared to go. And I'm frankly too scared to let them. We were being followed, they yelled at us. The girls are used to having a very busy mother who is lauded and mostly left alone to her laboratory. Now they have a mother who is called a foreign mistress and a conniving tramp.

HERTHA. Titanic bastards, all of them.

MARIE. An immigrant whore, a dirty Jew, a disgrace to her country, a—

HERTHA. Marie.

MARIE. —a disgrace to her *husband's memory.*

> *That was the biggest insult she weathered of course. Marie cracks again, trying to hold it together, not succeeding.*
> *The piano stops, perhaps Eve heard her mother and ran off.*

(To Eve in French.) *Tout va bien, mon ange, je vais bien, continue a jouer le piano si tu aimes.*

> *But the girl has run off.*

HERTHA. Alright. Alright.

> *Beat.*

First thing, I know you're not Jewish as much as we'd like to claim you. So the press are already lying and agitating.
Secondly, Pierre would understand. He would. It's been long enough, he'd want you to attempt some happiness which is exactly what you're doing with Paul. Your happiness would make him happy.

MARIE. On the good days I think you're right.

HERTHA. Well I am.

MARIE. On the bad days I think he'd hate me.

HERTHA. Marie. No. For what?

MARIE. For loving someone else. All this is some punishment for a wandering wife.

HERTHA. You're not wandering you're living, and frankly he's not! And punishment from whom? God? Really, if God has time to punish every person who finds complication in love he'd have time for nothing else.

MARIE. Well I'm certainly being punished for something.

HERTHA. I think it's what every woman is punished for: being alive and enjoying it. But that's why we married the men we did. They wanted us to live life.

MARIE. Every day since all this started, you know the first thing I think? Every morning I think: "Where is Pierre? I miss my friend. *I need my friend.*"

HERTHA. Now *Pierre* I'd back in a duel.
Many brilliant women don't marry good men but you did. That's how I knew you were wise as well as smart.
You've been through enough hardship to last ten lifetimes. And yet here you are. With more work to do, more to explore—

MARIE. But now I can't do any of that! Don't you see the severity of this. This country hates me, they'll take my funding, they'll take my students, the Radium Institute will vanish, the Academy will never let me in.

HERTHA. Yes but the Academy is full of men who were never going to let you in anyway.

MARIE. *(Rage.) It's a scientific goddamned Academy and I AM science in this goddamned country and* now they have the perfect excuse to erase me. "Defiler of French ideals."

HERTHA. *Oh come on,* sex is suddenly a controversy *in France*?!

MARIE. Paul *is* still married.

HERTHA. He's separated. He's getting a divorce you said.

MARIE. But he hasn't gotten it yet.

HERTHA. Well nothing's perfect.

MARIE. Perhaps I am a terrible person, we *were* sneaking around, he *does have* a wife.

HERTHA. And children.

MARIE. Yes, and children, and so do I, and they don't deserve all this, but now they live in a world that hates their mother.

HERTHA. The world doesn't hate you and neither do they. All they know is that they love you and you're hurting. I'm sure they just don't know what to do.

MARIE. When Pierre died, it was so much worse but we had support. Friends and colleagues. Everyone came to help. With this? They're scandalized. I disgust people. Everyone's abandoned me.

HERTHA. Except your British friend who shows up unannounced.

MARIE. Except for her. And with, what was it, a saber?

HERTHA. I love a battle, my dear. I'm here for the long haul. We'll outlast them.

MARIE. You know they may never let me in my lab again. That I cannot outlast.

HERTHA. Your lab? No. They can't do that can they?

MARIE. They hate me, they don't care, they'll take everything I have.

HERTHA. *They cannot take the lab of a Nobel Prize–winning physicist.*

MARIE. They can do whatever they want. And they don't want me. I used to be the most brilliant woman in Europe. Now?

HERTHA. Now you still are. You just had some very nice intimacies that I would like to hear all about when it's appropriate.

MARIE. *Oh, stop it. Stop.*

HERTHA. What? Men get to have sex all the time. They don't mind what Einstein does with his evenings, Einstein gets to keep his lab!

MARIE. Einstein doesn't have a lab he just wanders the halls looking a bit off.

HERTHA. That is not the point. The point is that *you* must be perfect and saintly and untouched, while the men do as they please. This is exactly what we're fighting for!

MARIE. I don't think my situation can be tied to suffrage.

HERTHA. Everything can be tied to suffrage!

MARIE. Hertha please.

HERTHA. There is no space for women to be people! That's what we're marching for. It's not just the vote, it's the freedom to be alive in this world without restriction. You aren't the most brilliant *woman* in the world, you're the most brilliant *scientist* in the world. And god if men don't simply love to knock an irreplaceable woman off her mark. That's what's happening to you, and it might not be the last time either. Which is why you must prove your resilience.

MARIE. I don't know if I am that.

HERTHA. *Goddammit yes you are.* You shoveled uranium ore for years in a shed, you can withstand this.

MARIE. Uranium was nicer. I want to disappear.

HERTHA. Marie.

MARIE. Or die.

HERTHA. *NO.* None of that talk. None of it.

MARIE. *(This is a fact.)* This is the end I think. I can't do this for much longer.

HERTHA. Yes you can, it's awful, I know that, but this is the worst part. You're in the middle of the worst of it, but that means it's the *middle.* It will get better, and all of this will pass, and you will have your lab back, and you will have your students, and you will have your science. It'll just take time. And it wouldn't hurt if you could stick it to them again and win another Nobel Prize or something.

MARIE. I actually…did.

HERTHA. …Sorry. What?

MARIE. They're giving me another one. For chemistry this time.

HERTHA. I'm sorry. You won *another* Nobel Prize?

MARIE. For the discovery of Radium and Polonium.

HERTHA. MARIE.

MARIE. Yes but—

HERTHA. No "but"! There is no "but"! MARIE! My god! You might've mentioned this earlier! I wouldn't have gone off on a feminist rant if I knew we had this to celebrate!

MARIE. I don't feel the least bit capable of celebration.

HERTHA. Who cares! I do! This is unprecedented! No one gets *two* prizes. No one gets *one* prize much less *two*! *In different fields!* This is absolutely tremendous!

MARIE. Yes well—

HERTHA. MARIE! You are a masterpiece in human form! I'll get champagne for us, and a cake for the girls.

MARIE. *They don't want me to come.*

Pause.

To the ceremony. The Nobel Committee asked me not to come.

HERTHA. Not to come accept the award they're giving you? Is this a joke?

MARIE. The scandal. I'm telling you it's worse than you think. My career is over.

HERTHA. *They don't get to decide that.*

MARIE. They don't want my presence tainting the ceremony.

HERTHA. *Well too bad, it's your ceremony.* And you can't tell me that every one of those men doesn't have some secret bullshit they wouldn't get away with if they were a woman, so they don't get to be righteous and they don't get to tell you what to do, *goddammit they do not.*

MARIE. That's what Albert said. Sort of.

> *Marie recovers a letter from Einstein, Hertha takes it…*

HERTHA. Einstein? Then he has taste and class as well as that ridiculous mustache.

"Dear Marie—I am so enraged by the base manner in which the public is daring to concern itself with you. I am compelled to tell you how much I admire your intellect, your drive, and your honesty. If the rabble continues to occupy itself with you then simply don't read that hogwash, but rather leave it to the reptile for whom it has been fabricated.—Yours, A. Einstein." My god, I've just fallen in love with him.

MARIE. It was nice to hear from him.

HERTHA. He always knows what to say, doesn't he. What's this bit at the end?

MARIE. Yes, he goes on about the statistical law of motion of the diatomic molecule.

HERTHA. Not sure I'd've put the hard physics in the postscript but I'm not Einstein.

MARIE. No one is.

HERTHA. You must go to that ceremony. Take your prize. It's *yours.*

MARIE. Yes but I don't think I care. It should make me happy, but I can't feel a thing.

HERTHA. Then they are winning and that is unacceptable. This is why I've come. No one could survive this kind of ignorant attack without friends. And distance.

MARIE. What do you mean distance?

HERTHA. I want you to come to England with me. Bring the girls, bring the nanny. I have a house on the coast. It's remote, it's beautiful, it's away from all this idiocy. You'll come.

MARIE. Oh…no, I can't.

HERTHA. And yet you will because you must. Get away from France. Come for a month or two or *ten*.

MARIE. I can barely walk down the street, much less travel to England.

HERTHA. What do you mean you can't walk?

MARIE. The pain, I have pain, my side, my back.

HERTHA. From stress or work.

MARIE. It's all stress or work!

HERTHA. Well there you go! That's why you need this! You'll use an alias. We'll travel at night. No one will know.

MARIE. You can't fix this.

HERTHA. I'm an electromechanical engineer and a mother of two, I can fix anything. You're coming. This is untenable here. Even for you.

MARIE. …Alright.

HERTHA. Oh. Really? You're really going to come?

MARIE. Well yes you just invited me.

HERTHA. I did but I never thought you'd actually do it.

MARIE. Did you not just invite me?

HERTHA. I did! Yes! *Good!* The girls will have so much fun, you can rest and recuperate and have a small sea in between you and France. You won't have to worry about a thing!

MARIE. Hertha.

HERTHA. Yes, my dear friend?

MARIE. *(Pure confession.)* I miss him so much.

HERTHA. I know. I know you do.
But, sorry, are we talking about Pierre or Paul?

MARIE. I don't know. It's all just agony.

> *Marie starts to break down again, Hertha catches her.*

HERTHA. You need to hear me say this. You do *not* in any way deserve this.

MARIE. Yes. I know. I know.
And I suppose he could divorce her.

HERTHA. He could. He might. He's gotta make it through that duel first but—

MARIE. *Oh god.*

HERTHA. Sorry. Don't think of that. Sorry. The truth is I don't really care about Paul at the moment, I only care about you and you are falling apart and the only way to recover is to start a new chapter. This is not the end of the book but we've got to start turning some pages.

MARIE. Yes. Yes.

HERTHA. Good. I'll have the house ready for us as soon as you return from the ceremony.

MARIE. I'm not going to the ceremony.

HERTHA. The hell you aren't. It's a Nobel goddamned Prize and they're going to put it in your goddamn hands.

MARIE. I don't want to be where I'm not wanted.

HERTHA. Who cares if you're wanted.
Here you are.

> *Blackout. A vial of radium glows brighter in the dark.*
> *Impossibly, we hear its tick tick tick.*

Scene 3

Marie on a boat.

MARIE. And then I am on a boat from Calais to Dover. I've told them my name is Sklodowska. That is, in fact, my name. The one I was born with decades ago before I married Pierre and became Curie, *Madame* Curie. Then *that* Madame Curie.
But with my old name, I am not her. I'm not anyone. I have shed myself. Half-life…

> *Tick tick tick…*
> *She listens to the radium. Smiles.*
> *Then the boat's horn announces their arrival.*

And now the boat is docking.
And I am waiting for—

> *The train station.*

HERTHA. *MARIE. Marie!*

MARIE. *(To herself.)* My friend. Who is here to greet me.

HERTHA. My dear you made it! Safe and sound and anonymous.

MARIE. *(To Hertha.)* Unless you keep yelling my name.

HERTHA. That's a fair point. I am not practiced in this much subterfuge. Come come come. The train down the coast isn't long. Welcome, my friend. Here you are.

> *Marie takes a breath.*
>
> *The breath becomes the steam of the train taking them away…*

Scene 4

Britain. Hertha's summer house—seaside, Highcliffe-on-Sea.
Calm, a stream trickling outside, trees rustling, a light breeze.
Hertha and Marie enter with luggage.

HERTHA. In you go, drop your things, there you are. Now. The house used to be an old water mill which is why it feels a bit like a barn, but I love the airiness of it, the windows, you can always hear the stream outside. It's truly a restorative sort of place. Before William died we'd come every summer. After he died this place saved my life.

MARIE. This place is…

HERTHA. Heaven. Isn't it? It's even better at dusk, or dawn. Anytime the light plays on it it's just magical.

MARIE. The light, you're right.

HERTHA. I know.

MARIE. The air too.

HERTHA. Sea air. It's almost sweet isn't it? It's the jasmine in the garden.

MARIE. That's it, jasmine. It smells like…almost like Poland.

HERTHA. Does it?

MARIE. The woods, the water. What a gift this is. Thank you.

HERTHA. No no, it is a gift to *me* to have you here. And soon your girls, and then my daughter in a few weeks, and what a wonder it will be to be together. Oh! Did you see the stream in the back? And the garden really is gloriously unkempt. The girls will love it. They'll get filthy. And the beach is just five minutes across that meadow. We can go every day if you like. The whole ocean laid out for us begging for a bath.

MARIE. Oh my.

HERTHA. I promise I'll stop talking so much, I'm just so glad you're here. Give me your coat. Give me your hat. You must be exhausted.

MARIE. A little, yes.

HERTHA. Well sit, my god! Or don't. Do whatever you like! Dance, prowl around naked—

MARIE. *Hertha.*

HERTHA. I mean it! Beat thy breast in the moonlight, or—you know—just take a nap.

MARIE. Pierre would've liked it here. He loved the sea.

HERTHA. William did too. You know I keep thinking he'll pop around the corner with his suit and towel, "Off to the beach, BG!"

MARIE. BG? What's BG?

HERTHA. That's what he called me, "Beautiful Genius."

MARIE. God I love him.

HERTHA. It does make marriage a bit easier when your husband calls you a genius all the time.

MARIE. He was such a good man. I liked him so much.

HERTHA. And he liked you too. He was the one who dragged me to that reception for you and Pierre, that first time. I wouldn't have gone except he said, "You've got to meet her, BG, you'll have so much in common." And then he tells me about Pierre and how he was just nominated for the Nobel, but he was going to refuse it if they didn't give the prize to you as well, and that he was standing up for his wife! And I said, "I want to meet her and ask her how she trained her husband so well!"

MARIE. I think you actually did ask me that.

HERTHA. I did! I wasn't joking!

MARIE. I remember you running across the room of men, charging at us to thank Pierre for being so valiant. He thought he was being arrested.

HERTHA. I do make a strong first impression.

MARIE. He loved you.

HERTHA. If we had more men like him in the world it would be a better place. At least the sciences would. You know I think they created their little Societies just to keep us out of them. You know they almost elected me once?

MARIE. *To the Royal Society? How?*

HERTHA. By accident.

MARIE. The French won't let me in and I've tried half a dozen times? How did you manage that?

HERTHA. Well I didn't say I managed it successfully.

MARIE. Oh no.

HERTHA. After my book on the electromechanics of arc lighting was published—to great acclaim among the five of us who care about the electromechanics of arc lighting—well someone nominated the great engineer Mr. Ayrton until they realized—

MARIE. That you are not Mr. Ayrton.

HERTHA. *Not* Mr. Ayrton, even though William insisted that we not work together to avoid this exact confusion. But as soon as they realized I was the Ayrton in the skirt they rejected me all over again.

MARIE. Because you're a woman.

HERTHA. Oh no, actually because I was a *married* woman—this was the worst part—married women are technically property of their husbands and not legal persons under the—you know—law, and "we can't have a person that doesn't legally exist elected to the Royal Society because that would be an existential contradiction we cannot abide even though, because we are physicists, we have no problem with the contradiction that light is both a wave and a particle."

MARIE. Science would be so much better without all the scientists.

HERTHA. Can you imagine telling Darwin he can't come to the meeting because he's married?

MARIE. I can't.

HERTHA. Because you're a reasonable person. God the shit we put up with to have a thought.

MARIE. It is exhausting.

HERTHA. For a moment after Barbara was born I was sad I had a daughter thinking of all the hypocrisy I'd have to explain to her.

MARIE. I know. How are your girls?

HERTHA. They're fabulous! Barbie's in jail, and I couldn't be happier.

MARIE. Jail? What? Why?

HERTHA. Suffrage protests. There were thousands of us and it was glorious. The police are vicious these days, granted there has been lots of smashing. Windows, storefronts. When Parliament defeated our bill it sent a bolt of rage through us all and we took to the streets. Barbara was the loudest, because the Ayrton girls only have one volume, so they spotted her right away.

MARIE. Are you not at all worried?

HERTHA. Oh no, she's fine. She's in with all my favorite people.

MARIE. Well I'm glad they didn't take you *both*.

HERTHA. Yes, they know better now. They used to nab me first, but I'm a terribly annoying prisoner and I think it dulled the fun for the guards to have me yelling and singing and spitting.

MARIE. Spitting? My god.

HERTHA. You use what you can. But I could be of more use outside. Someone's got to be ready for them when they're released. The ladies starve themselves you see, so they're all frail as kittens after a few weeks in there—and when the guards toss them out everyone heads to my house to be fattened up so they can go back to protesting and get arrested all over again.

MARIE. My goodness what courage. I don't know how you do it.

HERTHA. Well, women are not taught how to defend ourselves. Only how to protect our children. But I have daughters, you see, so that's exactly what I'm doing.

> *Marie smiles then—winces, tries to breathe through the pain.*

What's wrong? Marie.

MARIE. I'm fine.

HERTHA. No you're not, what's going on?

MARIE. I'm alright. I'm just tired.

HERTHA. There's a good doctor in town, not far at all if you want.

MARIE. I just need to be still for a moment. It passes. I don't know what triggers it but it passes.

HERTHA. Well that's a very general analysis for the foremost scientist in Europe.

MARIE. Stress doesn't help. That I know.

HERTHA. Ah. Well. That's what this summer is entirely about. Rest, my friend. You're safe here. You're free.

MARIE. Thank you.

Thank you.

Thank you.

> *Marie bursts into tears with that last utterance.*
> *She's not one to weep openly but she is now. Can't help it, can't stop it.*
>
> *Hertha holds her.*

HERTHA. Oh my dear friend. No one is built for this.

> *But suddenly Marie isn't sad, she's fucking furious. She rages with—*

MARIE. Those sick, sick, awful snakes—those writers, those men, they wouldn't leave me alone, it's my life, it's mine, how dare you. God I hate them. I've tried to be above it, I've tried. But I hate them so much and I wish them the exact pain I feel. Feel this pain, feel it like I do and then write your shitty little columns from the moral high ground. *How dare you.* Grinning and laughing—you know they laughed, you know they did. Never, never would they do that to a man.

HERTHA. No they would not. They would've taken him out for drinks.

MARIE. And her? Her I hate specifically because she did all this— she sent those letters—*our letters*—to the press. She drummed up this whole thing, and not because she loves him but because she wants to ruin him, and ruin me, and it's worked. And I miss him and I'm furious that I miss him and I love him and I'm furious that I love him. And she gets to have him and I don't. Why do we ruin each other? Why do I do this to myself again and again.

HERTHA. To yourself? No.

MARIE. *Yes.* Everyone I love…I lose. Everyone.

HERTHA. But you know you can't control that. Love wounds us. That's how you know it mattered at all. You have your girls.

MARIE. And when I look at them I think of all the pain they'll face in this life, and all the idiocy and it breaks my heart again.

HERTHA. My mother would say, "Sarah, God made women stronger than the world they're in, you'll be fine." I know you loved him, but you know the truth and you are strong enough to bear it: What you had cannot come back. You know that.

Pause. Marie hears this. It's hard to hear.

MARIE. Your name is Sarah?

HERTHA. What? Oh. Yes. Well, it used to be.

MARIE. Sarah is such a plain name for you.

HERTHA. Which is why I changed it. My mother called me Sarah but it never fit me.

MARIE. My mother called me Manya.

HERTHA. Manya! Ohh I love it. I can just see baby Manya picking flowers in the fields.

MARIE. I can't believe I never knew your real name.

HERTHA. Sarah Marks, with a little reinvention and one marriage, became Hertha Ayrton. I found my first name in a poem, and my last name in a man. My mother hated both.

MARIE. Which poem gave you Hertha?

HERTHA. Algernon Swinburne. He wrote this extraordinary poem and that was the title, "Hertha," and when I read it I thought, "My god, this is the secret truth of the universe."

MARIE. That sounds like physics not poetry.

HERTHA. Oh I think it all comes from the same spring. I was in love with literature before I found science and Swinburne wrote the whole poem in the voice of a woman—a goddess—Mother Nature herself, and she says, "I am earth, I am time, I am everything," and it…it shook me. It still does.

MARIE. I don't think I've ever been shaken by a poem,

HERTHA. *(Diving into the poem.)*
"I am that which began;
Out of me the years roll;
Out of me God and man;
I am equal and whole;
God changes, and man, and the form of them bodily; I am the soul."

MARIE. Oh my.

HERTHA.
"Before ever land was,
Before ever the sea,
Or soft hair of the grass,
Or fair limbs of the tree,
Or the fresh-coloured fruit of my branches, I was, and thy soul was
    in me."

> *Beat, awe.*

Isn't it wonderful?

MARIE. "I am that which began…"

HERTHA. And the thing goes on for two dozen verses. The declaration of it is so—I don't know—unstoppable. "I am, I am" over and over. Honestly, *that's* the part that made me change my name. As a girl from a poor family, Jewish family, very religious, eldest daughter taking care of everyone's needs but my own, longing to be free, to study, to live my life, I needed to say who *I was.* I'd never done it before. "I am not this girl you think I am, I am this, I am Hertha." My mother hated it so much, she refused to speak to me. But, thank you Algernon, it changed my entire life when I claimed who I was.

MARIE. And who was that?

HERTHA. A woman who knew her worth. I saw that same woman in you the first night we talked. I said I know exactly who that is. She's got a fire like I do.

MARIE. And…do I, do I still?

HERTHA. Of course you do.

MARIE. Of course I do. But then… I don't think that's true. I don't think it's possible. I know I am not the same, I've been frankly gutted by all this and I don't know exactly what's left.

HERTHA. What's left is a brilliant woman, a strong woman—

MARIE. What's left is a wife with no husband, a lover with no love, a scientist with no science, what else? An experimentalist with no lab, a woman with no country, no reputation, no future, my children must think I'm horrible, certainly their nanny does. Is there anything else? I don't think so. What does that leave? Who does that leave?

HERTHA. I don't know.

MARIE. Who does that leave?

HERTHA. I don't know what you're after—

MARIE. I don't know what's left. I don't know what is left of me or for me.

HERTHA. What's left is Science and Nature and the secrets of the universe. They cannot take that from you.

MARIE. Nature? Nature's as heartless as they come. I envy her.

HERTHA. You don't want to be heartless.

MARIE. Oh yes I do. For once in my life I would *love* to be just heartless enough to survive a day without weeping at the thought of what I had, what I lost. I would love that. Because love is a terrible thing to do to people. So much pain. Hearts crushed all the time, all over the world. And it's unnecessary, you know. Love. We don't need it. Birds don't need it. Trees, fish. All other life on earth does just fine without it. Nature is perfectly heartless. So is science. That's why I like it.

HERTHA. I don't like the idea of science being heartless. It takes heart to question the nature of things.

MARIE. I think we'd all have much more time to question the nature of things if we weren't so busy loving and hating each other.

HERTHA. But if we stopped feeling, would we lift our eyes for a moment and wonder about anything bigger than ourselves? That's what we do when we ask Mother Nature a question. That's what no other animal does but us. Science lifts us above ourselves, the *act* of it, the wonder, the awe—

MARIE. *There is no wonder left in me, there's nothing, I feel nothing because they've stripped me of myself to the point that I do not know who I am. I don't know, I don't know. I DON'T KNOW, I DON'T KNOW, I DON'T KNOW.*

> *Hertha flings open the great windowed door to the outside,*
> *The sound of the sea and the wind rush in. It's loud.*
> *She contends with the sound by yelling into the wind out*
> *the window.*
> *Marie watches in awe.*

HERTHA.
"I am that which began;
Out of me the years roll;
Out of me God and man;
I am equal and whole;
God changes, and man, and the form of them bodily; I am the soul."

> *Hertha shuts the door, the waves and wind sound vanish as the scene ends.*

Scene 5

Marie's ode to the night.

> *At night, alone, still shaking from…from what? Fear? Anger? She takes out her vial. The tick…*

MARIE. I… I…
I can't breathe.
Can't catch my—my breath. Like I'm drowning in air.
But then I take out the vial. I stare back, that glow. You can't see it during the day of course. But at night the darkness shows you what's been there the whole time. The glow, the gaze, in my hand, by my side.
This is what's left of me.
I grip it, there is a warmth. The very smallest fire, but I feel it.
It's there.
Thank god it's there.

> *She grips the vial like it's the thing saving her life.*
> *She holds it and her breath steadies. She takes a good breath at last.*
>
> *The tick vanishes.*

Scene 6

Bird song, seabirds, morning.
They walk to the shore.
The ocean slushes the sand.
The wind is light but constant. It's glorious.

HERTHA. I must say I'm profoundly proud of myself.

MARIE. This is unsurprising.

HERTHA. I'm hiding the greatest mind in the world at my summer house and no one knows! The woman all those papers are dying to photograph, all those hungry eyes looking out for you and I've tricked them so thoroughly that we can walk to the ocean for a picnic supper like we were absolutely no one of consequence. It tickles me so fully I can't stop smiling. Would you like a sandwich? I've got cucumber.

MARIE. Thank you, no.

HERTHA. How about a dip?

MARIE. A dip?

HERTHA. A dip.

MARIE. A dip is…an activity or a food?

HERTHA. A dip in the water, in the ocean. Let's go bathing!

MARIE. Oh. No no no.

HERTHA. It feels wonderful, I promise.

MARIE. No I couldn't, I can't.

HERTHA. Of course you can, it's a beach, it's what people do.

MARIE. I don't feel that strong today. Once the girls arrive. Perhaps.

HERTHA. Alright. I do love a perhaps.

MARIE. I know you do.

HERTHA. A whole world out there, unknowable if you stay on the shore.

MARIE. I know what you're doing, I'm not going in. And you studied the shore more than anyone. Don't tell me how boring the shore is.

HERTHA. Just because I studied it at an inane level of detail doesn't make it any less boring. Come on.

MARIE. *(Teasing her.)* No no, I'm with the foremost expert on sand in the world, why go into the water and waste all that expertise.

HERTHA. I didn't study *sand in general*, I studied *ripples in the sand*. Fluid dynamics, wave mechanics. The mathematics is very hard.

MARIE. I know it is.

HERTHA. There's a lot of maths in one little wave. I mean I wasn't discovering a new planet but the physics was difficult enough to force them to give me that damn Hughes Medal.

MARIE. It's a very handsome medal that one.

HERTHA. Isn't it? I'm quite proud of that medal in no small part because of all the men that didn't want me to have it. But I do wish they'd put something more impressive on the face of it, you know. All this fuss and the gold and in the end it's just a little man with a mustache.

MARIE. The Nobel is a little man with a mustache as well.

HERTHA. We should get them together and they can all have a little meeting.
Come on. Let's go in. Just to your ankles? Your toes?

MARIE. No, I said no, I don't like the cold, or the wet, or the fashion of ladies' swimwear, and I don't want to because I—I…I have a letter.

HERTHA. Sorry. A letter? A letter prevents you from bathing?

MARIE. Yes. No. I have a letter, in my pocket, it's from Paul, I'm not going in.

HERTHA. Wait wait wait, how do you have a letter from Paul? No one's supposed to know you're here.

MARIE. They don't. He sent it before I left but I'm too terrified to open it. I can't open it, I can't part from it, I'm at a loss.

HERTHA. Let me, would you.

MARIE. No. There's some kind of peace to being in between results that I quite like.

HERTHA. Give it.

MARIE. No.

HERTHA. Marie.

MARIE. No.

HERTHA. If you do it then it's done and if it's lovely we'll laugh and if it's infuriating we'll rip it up and throw it in the water and wish him a plague of some sort.

MARIE. Well I don't want him to die. Unless it's of heartbreak. He can die of heartbreak.

> *Marie hands her the letter. Hertha opens it.*

HERTHA. Well he obviously loves you.

MARIE. Oh god.

HERTHA. And he is very sorry and very worried about you and…

MARIE. What.

HERTHA. Oh. Well. He finally proposed a divorce.

MARIE. *He's getting a divorce? When? When is that happening? I should go back. He has no idea where I am.*

HERTHA. Wait now, just…

MARIE. What. Whatwhatwhat.

HERTHA. He says he's not leaving the children. And not leaving their house.

MARIE. Not leaving the house he lives in *with her*? What kind of divorce is that?

HERTHA. A very symbolic one. Oh shit she's pregnant.

> *That lands like a boulder on Marie's chest.*

MARIE. She's…she's pregnant?

HERTHA. He says he doesn't altogether believe her but—Oh god.

MARIE. His wife is…

HERTHA. What an idiot.   MARIE. Ohhhhhhkay.
A coward and a fool and a dog.   That is…

> *What does Marie do here? I think she wordlessly, sound-lessly reclines all the way back to the ground, facing the sky. Or facing the sand?*
> *Whatever it is is full-bodied and very unexpected for Hertha.*

HERTHA. What's happening here, is this emotional or medical?

MARIE. *(Testing out the idea.)* Hmm.
What an interesting feeling.

HERTHA. Are you alright? I mean of course you're not. I'm so sorry.

MARIE. No actually I am alright. I think. It feels like—what does it feel like? A release.

HERTHA. Good. See, that's good.

MARIE. Oh no it's horrible, I feel absolutely awful and hate him and hate everything but I suppose… You can't hate a fact can you?

HERTHA. No you cannot.

> Pause. The sounds of the ocean.
> Marie breathes deep then chuckles at a memory.

MARIE. You know when all of this started and everyone was saying, "Oh not Madame Curie, not with Langevin, he's married! Oh no!" Einstein wrote a letter to a colleague and it got back to me. You know what he said?

HERTHA. Oh god, what.

MARIE. He said…"But she's too plain to give any real woman cause to worry."

HERTHA. No.

MARIE. He did.

HERTHA. *No.*

MARIE. He did. And I had a moment that I am quite familiar with wherein I smile and swallow insult just to make it go away. But then I thought, I might be plain but I'm certainly compelling enough to rent a secret flat and meet every night for years, *Albert.*

HERTHA. That you are! That's damn right you are!

> Pause. The waves, gulls, crunch of sand.

MARIE. Is the water cold?

HERTHA. I don't know. Are you going in?

MARIE. I don't know.

> They stand at the shore. A sudden decision.

Yes I am going in.

HERTHA. Alright.

MARIE. Yes I am. Hold these.

Marie takes off her shoes as fast as she can.

HERTHA. Well good lord, let me get you a suit at least.

MARIE. I don't need a suit. I'm going in like this.

HERTHA. You can't wear your dress.

MARIE. No one knows me here, no one cares.

HERTHA. *Marie* it'll get soaked, it'll get heavy.

MARIE. I don't care.

HERTHA. It could drag you down.

MARIE. Then I'll strip it off.

HERTHA. *Marie.*

MARIE. Throw it off, throw it away, I don't care.

HERTHA. *Wait—please be careful.*

Splash. Marie's feet hit the water.

MARIE. Not anymore.

Marie dives in as Hertha watches. Splash.

Scene 7

Marie's ode to the underwater.

Underwater she thinks this, whispered rapidly, rhythmically, tidally.
If we can…we hear the roar and the slush of going above and below the surface of the water; she's drowning…or she's free.

MARIE. Wet dress, drug down, wet dress, sink, salt, sink.
Underwater I am weightless, carried and currented and…cradled.
No thought.
No thinking.
Just…
Heaving with the chest of the world as she breathes for us all.

I am not in my element.
I am...
Underwater I am...
...
I am...that which...began...

> *Will she stay under? Is this the end?*
> *Massive breath as she surfaces.*
> *Ocean lapping and pouring around her.*
> *Seagulls. Life.*

Scene 8

Back at the house Marie and Hertha are out of breath laughing so hard. They are in robes with their soaking wet clothes on the floor.

HERTHA. Oh my god their faces! All those horrified children looking at us like sea beasts risen from the ocean floor!

MARIE. We must've looked like monsters.

HERTHA. Or mermaids!

MARIE. Or beached whales.

HERTHA. I think this is great for children. We will have given them stories to tell for decades to come.

MARIE. Nightmares! Nightmares for decades.

HERTHA. Then they'll have to toughen up because that was *real*. I haven't had that much fun in years. Which came after the terror of being quite sure that you were drowning out there.

MARIE. No no, it was so peaceful.

HERTHA. Not for me it wasn't! I dove in thinking I'd pull you out by your hair.

MARIE. Which you sort of did.

HERTHA. The looks on their faces.

MARIE. All those children.

HERTHA. And their mothers.

MARIE. And their *fathers*.

HERTHA. Alas! Alack! Wet women! That's actually a brilliant protest strategy. Hundreds of women show up completely soaked. Any manner of physical engagement by police will prove us 1) slippery 2) heavy 3) absolutely giddy at our disruption. My god, I have to write my daughter.

MARIE. Hertha…

HERTHA. Yes, darling.

> *Taking her time…*

MARIE. I…I'll be fine.

HERTHA. Uh huh.

MARIE. Without him. With my daughters and my work and my life on my own. I will be fine. I wanted you to know that.

> *Hertha hears this. Then—*

HERTHA. I had no doubt about your resilience. You are its very definition.

> *Marie hears this. Beat. Appreciation.*

MARIE. We should go swimming again tomorrow.

HERTHA. We should go every day for the rest of our lives. But first tea. I'll put on the kettle.

MARIE. Shall I take our wet things up to dry?

HERTHA. No no no, let me manage that.

MARIE. Oh I can do it.

HERTHA. No no, you sit and think of something remarkable. I'll be right back.

> *Clink. A glass vial falls to the floor.*

Oh! Your jewelry, dear—

> *Hertha picks it up, stops mid-sentence…chilled.*

MARIE. You know I've never been to a protest or to jail. I'm starting to feel like I'm missing out.

HERTHA. Marie.

MARIE. Your girls must explain the allure of organized rebellion when they arrive.

HERTHA. *Marie.* I believe this is your…vial.

MARIE. Oh yes, thank you. Thank goodness it didn't float off.

HERTHA. I thought we agreed to leave the Radium in Paris.

MARIE. Yes but this vial is always with me. I never leave it.

HERTHA. But I asked you to leave it.

MARIE. And I didn't because I never do. Is this really a problem?

HERTHA. The problem is, you don't tell me it's here?

MARIE. Why would I tell you everything in my luggage.

HERTHA. Because that's not just anything *and it's not in your luggage.* Your children are coming, my daughters are coming, *I am here and so is that and I don't like it.*

MARIE. *I'm not asking you to like it,* I like it, it's a rather big feature in my life, it reminds me of *my husband, so I'll thank you to give it back.*

HERTHA. *And I'll thank you to put it on a boat back to Paris, I don't want it in my house.*

MARIE. *WHY.*

HERTHA. Because it's…

> *She doesn't say "dangerous."*

It's an impressive thing but it's…
(Admitting.) I worry.
Your hands. Burned. Black, in places. You hide it but…I worry.

MARIE. About what exactly do you worry? Worry is not proof.

HERTHA. I know it's not, but this is a young field.

MARIE. So we are to fear it? You fear this?

HERTHA. No but we don't know everything about it, not even you!

MARIE. I know it stops cancer, is that not good enough for you?

HERTHA. If it's powerful enough to stop cancer, why the hell are they putting it in goddamn toothpaste.

MARIE. I didn't tell them to put it in toothpaste.

HERTHA. You didn't tell them anything! Creams, powders, women putting this on their faces, children drinking it in tonics! They would've listened to you if you would've told them that the science isn't ready.

MARIE. *The science is ready.*

HERTHA. *It's not, it's only been around a decade!*

MARIE. *You are not qualified to judge me.*

HERTHA. I'm not judging, I'm responding to the fact that you're sick all the time and I wonder what's to blame.

MARIE. You don't know what you're talking about.

HERTHA. I know that you've got burns on your hands, black patches on your skin, you've been ill since the moment we met, you can't breathe sometimes, you can't stand. When you went for your little swim I thought you would die because I've never seen you have to exert yourself for that long without collapsing. That is not everyone's burden, and this prolonged exposure to a substance with permeative energetic power might not be helping. Not everything in nature is good.

MARIE. You fear it.

HERTHA. Yes, I do.

MARIE. You fear *me?*

HERTHA. *What? No.* No.

MARIE. Yes, I know that voice, that look. It's a bit similar to the men chasing me down the street.

HERTHA. Oh piss off, Marie.

MARIE. *You trick me, invite me here.*

HERTHA. *This is not a trick, I am here for you.*

MARIE. *How could you possibly be and say that to me.*

HERTHA. *Because I see my friend dying in front of me.*

      Beat. Beat.

MARIE. Then I shall leave in the morning.

HERTHA. That's not what I meant.

MARIE. It's clear what you meant. I'll leave right now.

HERTHA. You can't leave now. Your dress.

MARIE. I don't care about the goddamned dress.

HERTHA. I'm trying to protect you.

MARIE. *You can't protect me.* I. Am. Alone.
In this, and in everything else.

HERTHA. I'm right here, Marie. And frankly I'm the only one left.

MARIE. STOP TRYING TO FIX ME.
You can't.
I'm not a little light bulb.
My vial.

HERTHA. No.

MARIE. Give it to me.

HERTHA. No.

MARIE. Hertha.

HERTHA. Did you try and kill yourself today in the water? Is that what you were doing?

> *Beat. Outrage.*

MARIE. I truly thought we were friends of a different sort.

HERTHA. *(Losing it, not being nice anymore.) So did I. I thought you were worth saving.*

MARIE. Excuse me.

HERTHA. *I am happy to repeat it at a louder volume.*

MARIE. *I don't need you to save me. I save myself, in spite of a world that denies me everything.*

HERTHA. *Oh yes, God help the woman who has two Nobel Prizes.*

MARIE. *(Losing it.)* You think you know me, you always think you know, but you don't. That first night we met, you run to me, across a room of men, I'm the only other woman in the place, trying to demand respect and you run to me, calling my name, like we're sisters. *We're not.*

HERTHA. *Alright.*

MARIE. *We're not.*

HERTHA. *Alright.*

MARIE. You never wanted to save me, you just wanted to *matter*.

> *Holy shit that was cruel. Hertha is gobsmacked.*

It's not my fault that you chose to waste your brain on small things.
It's not my fault you chose to study *ripples in the sand* instead of
something with any value in this world. That is not my fault.
Stop blaming me.
Stop following me.
Do better.

HERTHA. I hope that I'm wrong about that vial of radium around
your neck.

MARIE. You are.

> *Marie takes her things and exits before Hertha can even
> call out.*
> *Hertha is alone. She's gone.*
> *Hertha is furious and heartbroken and stews, slams some-
> thing, breaks something. She can't breathe, needs air, opens
> that window again, which lets in all the sounds of the play
> so far.*

Scene 9

> *The sound of the electric arc takes over—hisssssssss,*
> *The sound of the sea takes over,*
> *The sounds of that wind.*
>
> *Those sounds continue as, somewhere else, on a train platform…*
>
> *Marie struggles too. She is in physical pain as always,*
> *But more so it is her heart that is breaking; she regrets her
> outburst,*
> *She is alone.*
> *The sound of that ticking overwhelms her,*
> *The sound of a heart beating, of a train steaming by,*
> *The sound of glass breaking like it did when that mob came
> for her—*
>
> *Marie silences all this noise with her entrance right now—*

Scene 10

> *Marie bursts back in the door of the house—slam. The next day.*

MARIE. *Alright.* I do not want to apologize even though what you said was ridiculous, but you must know, I hope you know, that I don't think of you as some lesser woman, I don't think that, you're brilliant, you know you're brilliant, but you make me furious and I see now that's just how this relationship works.

HERTHA. Hello.

MARIE. Hello.

HERTHA. Thought you'd be in Paris by now.

MARIE. I'm not.

HERTHA. No you're not.

MARIE. I stayed at the inn by the station for the night.

HERTHA. And now you're back at my door?

MARIE. Yes I'm back, I'd like to come in.

HERTHA. Well bienvenue.

MARIE. I went to the train, got on the train, got *off* the train, couldn't sleep all night, couldn't eat.

HERTHA. The food at that inn is terrible. The woman's never heard of salt.

MARIE. I don't care about the food, I couldn't eat or sleep or leave because you said something that got me thinking, and I was thinking and thinking and now I'm here because I can't stop thinking about what you said.

HERTHA. Well sit down and tell me what the hell I said.

MARIE. I will not sit, I will never allow anyone to tell me what to do ever again.

HERTHA. Well I'm going to have a drink. I won't tell you to have

40

one with me but I'm just going to put the bottle right here and we'll see what happens.

MARIE. Alright.

HERTHA. Alright.

       Hertha opens the bottle and drinks.

MARIE. You said that I wasn't worth saving. That's what you said.

HERTHA. No I didn't.

MARIE. Yes you did.

HERTHA. No, I said, "I thought you were worth saving."

MARIE. But the implication was that I wasn't.

HERTHA. Implication isn't my problem. Are you?

MARIE. What?

HERTHA. Worth. Saving.

MARIE. Yes.

HERTHA. Alright then.

       Beat. Drink. Space and time.

MARIE. Are we going to apologize to each other or just move on?

HERTHA. I'm not really very sorry about anything.

MARIE. Neither am I.

HERTHA. Where's the vial?

MARIE. …I have a small lead-lined case in my trunk. It's in there.

HERTHA. …Fine.

MARIE. Good.

HERTHA. But alright, who just *has* a small lead-lined case in their trunk. Is it heavy?

MARIE. It's lead. Of course it's heavy.

HERTHA. I mean I assumed but I just work with sand, I don't do anything of value in this world.

MARIE. I'm sorry I said those things. They weren't true. I'm sorry I left.

HERTHA. To be honest I loved that part. Got to garden, clean up a bit, air out the radium in the sheets.

MARIE. You're right, let's not apologize.

> *Beat. What do they do now?*

Just pass the whiskey.

> *Clink! They both drink together.*

Scene 11

> *An hour later and they are quite drunk and speaking rapid French.*

MARIE. *Non Non Non! C'était merveilleux. Je suis si heureux que j'y suis allé!* [No, no, no! It was wonderful. I am so happy that I went!]

(English.) I'm saying that you were right!
I'm glad I went to the ceremony.

HERTHA. *Mais comment cela peut-il être vrai?* [But how can that be true?]

(English.) Oh come on—

HERTHA. I had to force you to go!

MARIE. Yes you did and I'm glad. It was fabulous! Can I not give you credit?

HERTHA. Not when you just said that you hated every minute of it!

MARIE. Well I did hate it until I gave my speech and told them all to fuck off.

HERTHA.
YOU DID NOT TELL THE NOBEL COMMITTEE TO FUCK OFF and I know because that would have been international news.

MARIE.
AlrightAlrightAlright…

MARIE. I did not say those words but it was in my voice and my… formidable eye contact.

HERTHA. You do have fabulous eye contact.

MARIE. Thank you very much. It makes the men soooo nervous.

HERTHA. And I'd wager a bit infatuated. That's what got them all so mad: "Why didn't she fall in love with me?"

MARIE. Did I tell you the real reason why they didn't want me to come? You'll love it.

HERTHA. I thought it was "the dignity of the occasion" or some horseshit like that.

MARIE. Oh no. The seating arrangements.

HERTHA. NO. What?

MARIE. It's an eleven-course meal, "Who shall we seat next to the harlot?" The King of Sweden?

HERTHA. Or better yet, his wife?

MARIE. It's an affair gentlemen, it's not contagious.

HERTHA. And they blame us for being hysterical.

MARIE. And they were! The little men with the clipboards were apoplectic! So of course—and I think you'd be very proud of me— before I left the ballroom I made a point of visiting every single table to thank them for coming to honor me.

HERTHA. I have quite truly never been more proud.

MARIE. Thank you very much.

HERTHA. God the amount of money I would have paid to see them squirming.

MARIE. It was incredibly satisfying. Pierre would have loved it.

HERTHA. Because he was a goddamned gentleman. May we have more men on this earth like him. And a few really handsome ones like Paul.

MARIE. WOULD YOU STOP TALKING ABOUT PAUL. I just got over this and you bring it up every second!

HERTHA. I'm just saying! I want to know more. You won't tell me!

HERTHA. You had a scandalous international love affair and I am a lonely widow now can we please discuss the sex.

MARIE. You're terrible, it was fabulous, leave me alone.

HERTHA. MarieMarieMarie wait, please, *what kind of fabulous* I need details, I need diagrams.

MARIE. Oh my god, stop it.

HERTHA. Only if you stop hogging the whiskey and tell me the fun stuff.

MARIE. HERE HERE HERE.

HERTHA. Come onnnnnnn.

MARIE. Alright, I don't know, it was… We were at the conference together in Brussels and we spent the day arguing about radon decay and we didn't really stop arguing until he was in my room at one A.M. and he said "I love you" and I said "I realize that now" and we agreed that it would be terribly complicated but we were beyond the point of caring and from that day on we tried not to spend a night apart. It wasn't wild, it was *real*.

HERTHA. *(Ruining her reflective moment.)* Lights on, hair down? Give me something.

MARIE. No, god, would you get a book. Why are you obsessing?

HERTHA. Because you're a rare specimen! Your lovers keep getting younger. That's not supposed to happen to women.

MARIE. I had *one* lover! One! Yours was more interesting than mine.

HERTHA. My what?

MARIE. When you met your husband! That was much more dramatic.

HERTHA. No it wasn't. Mother disapproved, I married him anyway, it was all very predictable.

MARIE. You went against your religion. William wasn't Jewish.

HERTHA. Neither was I at that point. Gave that up about the time I changed my name, which tells you all you need to know about my mother's mental health. William proposed, I accepted and I told my mother if she objected I'd choose him.

MARIE. Did she object?

HERTHA. Not once she met him! She loved him! It was all very sensible in the end, he was older, he was richer, he loved me to absolute bits and I him. The end.

MARIE. He was your professor!

HERTHA. Which makes me the smartest one in the class, what's your point?

MARIE. That what you had was way more important than whatever Paul and I had.

HERTHA. *You* had secret sex for years is what you had.

MARIE. Oh come on, I was cavorting!
(Like the following is a wonderful achievement.) You went to prison!

HERTHA. What's prison got to do with it? I thought we were getting to the nudity.

MARIE. Passion! The kind that really matters. You protested with your life for what you believe in.

HERTHA. So did you!

MARIE. No I didn't, I just fell in love with the wrong man.

HERTHA. Well sometimes love is protest. You defied their image of you, and you did it with exactly the kind of passion that makes them nervous. And you managed a bit of physics on the side. Good on you.

> *Beat, conceding.*

MARIE. Paul was very creative.

HERTHA. That's what I want to hear. Keep drinking.

> *Beat.*

MARIE. But you know what our passion truly is?

HERTHA. You and I?

MARIE. Yes. We love our lovers and we adore our children, but our life's passion…is proof.

HERTHA. Proof.

MARIE. Yes. Knowing what's true and proving it.
Peering for just a moment into the heart of the universe and snatching some truth before the curtain closes.

HERTHA. Mother Nature doesn't give you much but when she does?

MARIE. She gives you everything.

HERTHA. That. Is the greatest feeling in the world.

MARIE. God yes it is.

HERTHA. Although I really do love a summer nap with the windows open.

MARIE. Ooh yes that's a
very good feeling.
And my children laughing.
Nothing better.   HERTHA. Ah yes. Absolutely.
Perhaps them sleeping, all
splayed out like—

HERTHA. Like a dropped doll yes, sleeping children is a wonder of the world.

MARIE. And walking into one's laboratory knowing that it's yours.

HERTHA. Oh yes, a near perfect feeling.

MARIE. The stillness of things before work begins.

HERTHA. The calm, the refuge from all else.

MARIE. The potentiality.

HERTHA. Yes.

MARIE. The poise.

HERTHA. Yes.

MARIE. Then…after attempt and failure and idea and iteration…

HERTHA. The curtain opens, you have seconds to peer in, to find the truth, then proof.

MARIE. Then proof.

HERTHA. Proof is pure.

MARIE. Recognition is political. And proof can be yours alone, even for an hour knowing something that no one in the world knows but you.

HERTHA. God I love that feeling.

MARIE. God I love that feeling.

> *One more toast.*

To the Goddess of Proof and Wonder.

HERTHA. And Sleeping Children.
May we serve thee and know thee from now to eternity.

MARIE. (*"Cheers" in Polish.*) *Na Zdrowie.*

HERTHA. *Na Zdrowie.*

Clink! Drink…honesty.

MARIE. Do you think… Do you think they will ever let me live it down? All this?

HERTHA. You've already lived it down, they just have to catch up.

MARIE. I suppose I don't really care what they think as long as they let me work.

HERTHA. They don't *let you* do anything. If they say you can't show up, show up anyway. If they want to fight you for your power, you stand exactly where you are and draw the front line at your feet. We're women, we're always at the front line of something. And they've only succeeded at stopping you if you stop. So don't.
Or else I will come to your house and yell at you.

> *Pause.*

MARIE. You know I think you saved my life.

> *Hertha fully hears this. Takes it in.*

I needed this. A friend. Which would be you.

> *That meant so much.*

HERTHA. Of course it's me, who else would it be, Albert? It's not Albert. It's me.

MARIE. I'm trying to say thank you.

HERTHA. I know you are.

MARIE. Would you just let me be nice.

HERTHA. I will because I love you and we are goddesses of the god-damn earth.
If we want to be.

> *Breath, drink, blackout into—*

Marie's ode to this moment.

Small spot on Marie. Breathing deeply, in control, her old self, ready.
She retrieves the tube of radium from the lead case. Holds it.
Then locks the radium away again. Doesn't need it anymore. Stretches and rubs her aching hands. But she's going to be okay. She knows that now. It's true now.

She stands. She's ready. Blackout.

Scene 12

A week later...

We hear footsteps around the house, someone in the kitchen, children laughing and running around outside. Our two women are folding clothes or making sandwiches or some-thing beautifully domestic together. They are a team. They are a family.

HERTHA. God I do love a full house. Too much going on is just about right for me.

MARIE. The girls are so happy here running around like puppies.

HERTHA. We finally got Irene smiling. I thought she'd hold out on me for the whole summer.

MARIE. I think it was the maths lessons that did it. You spoke her language.

HERTHA. A little mathematics always cheers me up too.

MARIE. And you know for a known criminal, your Barbara is very good with children.

HERTHA. With *your* children she is. Most children give her hives. Me too actually. I've always enjoyed my children the older they got.

MARIE. Oh yes, I love them at every age, but I *like* them so much more now that they can pour their own milk and do their own physics.

HERTHA. I've only ever seen your Evie draw or play piano.

MARIE. Oh yes, Eve is all artist. Irene is all me.

HERTHA. What lucky girls to have a mother like you.

MARIE. I'd say the same for yours.

> *A door opens and little feet run in.*
> *Little Eve starts to play the piano... a waltz by Chopin, perhaps?*
> *It's obvious that she has talent.*

HERTHA. My word, I cannot fathom how good she is.

MARIE. I know. I told you.

HERTHA. Only seven and that good?

MARIE. She hates being complimented though. She can only compare herself to how she'll sound twenty years from now. She refuses to be told how good she is knowing how much better she could be.

HERTHA. Oh I think I like that. There's a fire in that kind of thinking. Though it does diminish the excellence of the present, doesn't it.

> *They listen to the piano…*
> *A moment for them to ponder big things in silence…*
> *Then Little Eve stops playing.*

MARIE. *Evie, mon ange. Tu continue a jouer!*

HERTHA. Yes, sweet thing, keep playing, we love it so.

> *She plays and plays.*
> *As the following progresses, Little Eve's playing gets better and better until it is quite masterful, as anyone's would be with the passage of time.*
> *Which is what we are witnessing: the future.*
> *A co-monologue as time passes rapidly, the two friends together through it all…*

MARIE. The summer.

HERTHA. This summer.

MARIE. We stay for the summer.

HERTHA. The summer of 1912, a perfect time.

MARIE. My daughters join me and I am the happiest I've been in years.

HERTHA. Her daughters are so much like her.

MARIE. Not my youngest.

HERTHA. Not Evie who thinks of nothing but music and books.

MARIE. My eldest.

HERTHA. Irene is her mirror image. A scientist's heart.

MARIE. We have such a lovely summer and then—

HERTHA. Head home.

MARIE. And then—

HERTHA. Time passes.

MARIE. I feel better, I feel worse. That nagging pain that won't subside—

HERTHA. And then—

MARIE. And then—

HERTHA. A war.

MARIE. A war.

HERTHA. A war begins.

MARIE. 1914.

HERTHA. 1914 and Europe loses its goddamn mind.

MARIE. June 28 the archduke is killed.

HERTHA. Austria declares war on Serbia.

MARIE. Germany declares war on Russia.

HERTHA. Then on France.

MARIE. Then invades Belgium.

HERTHA. Britain declares war on Germany,

MARIE. And bombs fall on Paris.

HERTHA. They're bombing Paris?! My god, *Marie*.

MARIE. I'm fine.

HERTHA. The girls? How are the girls?

MARIE. In the south, we're alright.

HERTHA. Thank god.

MARIE. You don't believe in God.

HERTHA. And this is goddamn why. You're sure you're alright?

MARIE. I will be if they keep their bombs away from my Institute.

HERTHA. You have to get out, the Germans are marching your way.

MARIE. I am keenly aware of this. We're taking the Radium to Bordeaux.

HERTHA. Who's we?

MARIE. Me, and one very heavy lead box.

HERTHA. Please be careful. My god, what is happening to this world?

MARIE. New Year's Day of 1915 I write to Paul.

HERTHA. *Yes. That* Paul.

MARIE. "I am resolved to put all my strength at the service of my adopted country of France."

HERTHA. That would be the country that just got done dragging her name through the mud. She offered the French government her Nobel Prizes.

MARIE. To melt down the gold for the war effort.

HERTHA. Don't give them your medals, for god's sake!

MARIE. I don't need them. I know what I did.

HERTHA. They didn't take her medals.

MARIE. Suit yourself.

HERTHA. Then she had a better idea.

MARIE. I have a better idea.

HERTHA. She always does. And this one could save lives by the millions.

MARIE. I thought…how could radiation be of use to soldiers at the front.

HERTHA. X-rays.

MARIE. X-rays.

HERTHA. Which have been around for a good two decades but her invention was so simple yet absolutely unheard of:

MARIE. *Mobile* X-rays.

HERTHA. Isn't that fabulous.

MARIE. I remembered what you said, "Women are always at the frontlines of something."

HERTHA. I didn't mean it literally.

MARIE. Why can't we make X-rays portable?

HERTHA. Why *can't* we make them portable?

MARIE. No reason. Modify an ambulance, use the car's engine to power it and we can take it anywhere.

HERTHA. See. It's brilliant.

MARIE. I convince the government to let me design and build the X-ray cars.

HERTHA. But who will drive them?

MARIE. I will, if I have to.

HERTHA. And she does. She doesn't just design them *she drives them herself.* She even studied basic anatomy.

MARIE. In case someone needs help with the surgery.

HERTHA. And they did.

MARIE. I prefer physics.

HERTHA. This woman and her two Nobel Prizes drives a god-damned ambulance in the middle of a world war—

MARIE. —I told you they didn't want the prizes—

HERTHA. —to carry an invention of her own making to help wounded soldiers in a country that just finished calling her "foreign trash." I would not have had the grace nor the grit.

MARIE. Yes you would.

HERTHA. She needed an assistant.

MARIE. Someone to help me drive the car, work with machines, interpret the scans.

HERTHA. Her daughter.

MARIE. My daughter.

HERTHA. Irene.

MARIE. My daughter and I. We took those cars to the front ourselves.

HERTHA. Something like a million soldiers were treated on the fields in those Petite Curies.

MARIE. That's what they call the cars—

HERTHA. —Not the women—

MARIE. "Little Curies."

HERTHA. "Little Curies." Here to save your leg.

MARIE. Or life.

HERTHA. Or the very fate of a non-fascist Europe.

MARIE. That's a bit much.

HERTHA. Not by my estimation.

MARIE. Hertha had an idea too.

HERTHA. Yes I did. We're not in the era of horses and cannons anymore. Chemical warfare has been born.

MARIE. April 1915. Allied troops await an onslaught of German soldiers, but instead…

HERTHA. A yellow gas lurches across the field and pools into their trenches. One hundred fifty tons of chlorine gas begin to scorch their lungs from the inside.

MARIE. What weapon can stop that?

HERTHA. We don't need another weapon we need…a fan.

MARIE. A fan.

HERTHA. Yes a fan, for fanning, get the gas out of the trenches or else it kills half your regiment in minutes.

MARIE. So they wave some leaves around, why does this require science?

HERTHA. Because you need a *proper* fan not *any* fan, which is why it's very convenient that I wrote an entire treatise on fluid dynamics.

MARIE. Waves aren't just for water, and ripples aren't just for sand.

HERTHA. Airflow, ladies and gentlemen! Wave a fan willy nilly and the gas will just spread through the whole trench. But if you know what you're doing and use the right equipment the gas is gone in seconds.

MARIE. Gone.

HERTHA. *Gone.*

MARIE. You should make that fan.

HERTHA. I should.

MARIE. She did.
And they should make sure everyone in the allied forces has one.

HERTHA. That's the idea.

MARIE. The British military did not think that was the idea and turned her away.

HERTHA. *Sightless sons of cows.*

MARIE. Then they tried the damn thing.

HERTHA. And it worked.

MARIE. And they distributed a hundred thousand Ayrton Fans to soldiers across the continent.

HERTHA. Even the Americans wanted them.

MARIE. And that's saying something.

>*They both stop, breathe.*

HERTHA. Now I'm not saying that we won the war for the Allies.

MARIE. But we helped.

HERTHA. Good work, Madame Curie.

MARIE. Good work, Mrs. Ayrton.

>*Beat.*

HERTHA. When the war is over I vote in my home country for the first time in my life.

MARIE. When the war is over I go back to work. I find myself with funding, public gratitude, and freedom.

HERTHA. When the war is over I find myself with…a grandson. I cannot get enough of him. He is the light of my life and currently sleeping the sleep of the wise and well-fed in his cart on the lawn like a rosy little cherub.

MARIE. This is the last letter I receive from you.

HERTHA. It is nearly the last letter I write.

MARIE. Hertha, what's going on?

HERTHA. It is August of 1923 and…I'm dying. Which is an odd thing to say out loud.

MARIE. *What.* What happened? What can we do?

HERTHA. Nothing. Blood poisoning. Spider bite they think.

MARIE. No.

HERTHA. Alas.

MARIE. *Hertha.*

HERTHA. There's nothing to be done.

MARIE. There's always something to be done. I'm coming.

HERTHA. Marie.

MARIE. *I'm coming.*

HERTHA. Marie.

MARIE. *Do not die, I'm coming.* I catch a train, I catch a boat, *I'm coming—*

HERTHA. I try and write one more letter to you—

MARIE. This is my ode to you. Wild thing. Woman. Examiner of Nature. Mother of Rebels.

HERTHA. I am trying to say thank you and I know you and I love you.

MARIE. Suffrage Fighter, Journey Maker, Engineer of the Electric.

HERTHA. But I can barely hold the pen—

MARIE. Wielder of Sabers. Saver of Souls.

HERTHA. So my daughter writes for me—

MARIE. Goddess of wonder and proof—

HERTHA. A letter that would have told you that on a warm day in August.

MARIE. *I'm coming, I'm almost there.*

HERTHA. The light on the ceiling bouncing around like—

MARIE. Hertha, wait—

HERTHA. Like waves that go on and on and on—

MARIE. I'm here. *I'm here.*

HERTHA. And on and on and on…

 Hertha fades away. Absence. Marie alone.

MARIE. No. Nonono. I know you. You're here, you're right here, I know you, you're going to fling open a door and come in and start yelling or telling me something wonderful.
I know you, I know you…and…

 Marie is hit with grief anew. Alone. Silence.

MARIE. …And you were right. I outlasted them. The gossips, the outrage. Who even remembers it now. Something so powerful diminished by time. But then again isn't that the story of the world. I work and work. I travel the world. The girls come with me. The American president hosts me. I am a member of the League of Nations with Einstein. The Radium Institute grows and grows. I am still sick, always sick, but I accept this life because it is mine. Because you gave it back to me.
The world is bigger than both of us. But for that summer it wasn't. Thank god it wasn't.

> *Marie is standing on the ocean shore.*

And now I stand on that same shore on which we stood all those years ago. Of course it's different now. The wind annoys me, the salt stings, the sun is too bright.

> *And then, Hertha is beside her.*

HERTHA. Now now. Don't get mad at the ocean. It didn't do any-thing to you.

MARIE. You would say.
"I'm not mad at the ocean I'm just tired," I would say.

HERTHA. "Good lord, everyone's tired."

MARIE. You would say.

HERTHA. "I'm dead and I'm tired."

MARIE. And it has been a decade and I still find myself in conver-sation with you.
A decade and I still want to ask, "Where have you gone, friend?" I think of you so often. You could've lived another thirty years. You should've.

HERTHA. Talk to the spider not to me.

MARIE. *You should've, you could've.*

HERTHA. *(Knows this is big news, carefully.)* Well then…so should you have.

> *Pause. Did she hear that right?*

MARIE. What?

>	*Beat.*

HERTHA. You should've lived longer than sixty-six. I blame the Radium. Everyone does.

MARIE. Sixty-six…

HERTHA. You are standing on a shore, Manya.

MARIE. I know that of course I am.

HERTHA. An unknown ocean in front of you.

MARIE. I know where I am, I know this place.

HERTHA. You don't actually. No one does…until right about this moment. When they realize that they are dying. And you are.

>	*Marie is thunderstruck.*

And in your very last moment, this moment, you ask Mother Nature

MARIE. What is true?

HERTHA. There is no seaside.

>	*The ocean vanishes.*

You are dying in a large room, windows open. Irene is beside you, Eve is too. She's playing piano.

>	*Piano plays again, so distant.*

You are now at the limit, my friend. The point where so much is changed, you are something else altogether.

MARIE. Half-life.

HERTHA. Yes.

MARIE. Mine.

HERTHA. Yes.

MARIE. Radium to Radon, to Polonium, to Lead to—

HERTHA. To You. Manya. Child of wonder.

MARIE. And you're with me?

HERTHA. I always have been.

MARIE. And my girls?

HERTHA. A scientist and a pianist. One wins a Nobel Prize like you, the other plays Carnegie Hall and lives to one hundred and two.

MARIE. And the…the work I did?

HERTHA. It is respected. And feared.

> *Silence. Marie breathes, steadies. Then Marie is ready.*

MARIE. Good. Alright then. One more experiment left. One more…

> *Breath, wind, breath, storm, tick, hiss, surge, clink!*
> *The women hold hands through the sounds, through the storm.*
>
> *Gasp.*
>
> *And disappear.*
>
> *Blackout.*

End of Play

PROPERTY LIST

(Use this space to create props lists for your production)

SOUND EFFECTS
(Use this space to create sound effects lists for your production)

Dear reader,

Thank you for supporting playwrights by purchasing this acting edition! You may not know that Dramatists Play Service was founded, in 1936, by the Dramatists Guild and a number of prominent play agents to protect the rights and interests of playwrights. To this day, we are still a small company committed to our partnership with the Guild, and by proxy all playwrights, established and aspiring, working in the English language.

Because of our status as a small, independent publisher, we respectfully reiterate that this text may not be distributed or copied in any way, or uploaded to any file-sharing sites, including ones you might think are private. Photocopying or electronically distributing books means both DPS and the playwright are not paid for the work, and that ultimately hurts playwrights everywhere, as our profits are shared with the Guild.

We also hope you want to perform this play! Plays are wonderful to read, but even better when seen. If you are interested in performing or producing the play, please be aware that performance rights must be obtained through Dramatists Play Service. This is true for *any* public performance, even if no one is getting paid or admission is not being charged. Again, playwrights often make their sole living from performance royalties, so performing plays without paying the royalty is ultimately a loss for a real writer.

This acting edition is the **only approved text for performance**. There may be other editions of the play available for sale from other publishers, but DPS has worked closely with the playwright to ensure this published text reflects their desired text of all future productions. If you have purchased a revised edition (sometimes referred to as other types of editions, like "Broadway Edition," or "[Year] Edition"), that is the only edition you may use for performance, unless explicitly stated in writing by Dramatists Play Service.

Finally, this script cannot be changed without written permission from Dramatists Play Service. If a production intends to change the script in any way—including casting against the writer's intentions for characters, removing or changing "bad" words, or making other cuts however small—without permission, they are breaking the law. And, perhaps more importantly, changing an artist's work. Please don't do that!

We are thrilled that this play has made it into your hands. We hope you love it as much as we do, and thank you for helping us keep the American theater alive and vital.

Note on Songs/Recordings, Images, or Other Production Design Elements

Be advised that Concord Theatricals neither holds the rights to nor grants permission to use any songs, recordings, images, or other design elements mentioned in the play. It is the sole responsibility of the producing theater/organization to obtain permission of the copyright owner(s) for any such use. Additional royalty fees may apply for the right to use copyrighted materials.

For any songs/recordings, images, or other design elements mentioned in the play, works in the public domain may be substituted. It is the producing theater/organization's sole responsibility to ensure the substituted work is indeed in the public domain. Concord Theatricals cannot advise as to whether or not a song/arrangement/recording, image, or other design element is in the public domain.